PowerPhonics™

Huge Animals

Learning the Long U Sound

Pam Vastola

The Rosen Publishing Group's
PowerKids Press™
New York

Some animals are huge.

ephant

bear

whale

3

An elephant is huge.

5

An elephant has huge ears.

7

A baby elephant is cute!

A bear is huge.

A bear has huge paws.

13

A baby bear is cute!

A whale is huge.

17

A whale has a huge tail.

18

19

A baby whale is cute!

Word List

cute

huge

Instructional Guide

Note to Instructors:
One of the essential skills that enable a young child to read is the ability to associate letter-sound symbols and blend these sounds to form words. Phonics instruction can teach children a system that will help them decode unfamiliar words and, in turn, enhance their word-recognition skills. We offer a phonics-based series of books that are easy to read and understand. Each book pairs words and pictures that reinforce specific phonetic sounds in a logical sequence. Topics are based on curriculum goals appropriate for early readers in the areas of science, social studies, and health.

Letter/Sound: long u – List and pronounce words having the **long u** sound: *blue, cube, cute, fuse, glue, tune, use, June, July,* etc. Encourage the child to add words to the list. Have them find the longest word, the shortest word, words with the same initial consonant, etc. Ask the child to underline **long u** in each word.

Phonics Activities: On a chalkboard or dry-erase board, write the following words for the child to decode and use in sentences: *cub, cut, hug, us.* Have the child underline **short u** in each word. Add **e** to the end of each word. Ask the child to find the two words that appeared in *Huge Animals.* Lead them to conclude that all the words now have the **long u** as well as a **silent e**. After decoding the words, have the child underline the **long u** and circle the **silent e** in each of them.

- List the following words: *tune, June, blue, glue, rule, mule.* Have the child tell how these words are like those in the previous activity. Have them underline **long u** and circle the ending **e** in each word. Ask them to decode the words and use them in sentences.

- Write the following words on the chalkboard or dry-erase board: *bake, blue, cube, need, see, make, goat, hide, time, tune, June, keep, shine, late, gold, find,* etc. Ask the child to read the words and talk about the long vowel sound they hear in each one. Make five columns, one for each of the vowel sounds (**a, e, i, o, u**). Have the child write words from the list under the appropriate columns and underline the letters that make the long vowel sound in each.

Additional Resources:
- Berman, Ruth, and Lynn M. Stone. *Fishing Bears.* Minneapolis, MN: The Lerner Publishing Group, 1998.
- Davies, Nicola. *Big Blue Whale.* Cambridge, MA: Candlewick Press, 1997.
- Denis-Huot, Christine, and Michel Denis-Huot. *The Elephant: Peaceful Giant.* Watertown, MA: Charlesbridge Publishing, Inc., 1992.
- Kulling, Monica. *Elephants: Life in the Wild.* New York: Golden Books Publishing Company, Inc., 2000.

2/05

Published in 2002 by The Rosen Publishing Group, Inc.
29 East 21st Street, New York, NY 10010

Book Design: Haley Wilson

Photo Credits: Cover © Stan Osolinski/FPG International; pp. 3 (upper left), 5 © Sneesby/Wilkins/Animals Animals; pp. 3 (upper right), 11 © Zig Leszczynski/ Animals Animals; pp. 3 (bottom), 17 © VCG/FPG International; p. 7 © Richard Sobol/Animals Animals; p. 9 © J & B Photographers/Animals Animals; p. 13 © Donna Ikenberry/Animals Animals; p. 15 © Joe McDonald/Animals Animals; pp. 19, 21 © Planet Earth Productions/FPG International.

Library of Congress Cataloging-in-Publication Data

Vastola, Pam.
  Huge animals : learning the long U sound / Pam Vastola.— 1st ed.
     p. cm. — (Power phonics/phonics for the real world)
  ISBN 0-8239-5931-7 (lib. bdg. : alk. paper)
  ISBN 0-8239-8276-9 (pbk. : alk. paper)
  6-pack ISBN 0-8239-9244-6
  1. Mammals—Juvenile literature. 2. English
language—Vowels—Juvenile literature. [1. Elephants. 2. Bears.
3. Whales.] I. Title. II. Series.
  QL706.2 .V37 2001
  599—dc21
                                          2001000380

Manufactured in the United States of America